Insomnia

Insomnia

Poems

John Kinsella

W. W. NORTON & COMPANY
Independent Publishers Since 1923

For information about permission to reproduce selections from this book, write to
Permissions, W. W. Norton & Company, Inc., 500 Fifth Avenue, New York, NY 10110

For information about special discounts for bulk purchases, please contact
W. W. Norton Special Sales at specialsales@wwnorton.com or 800-233-4830

Manufacturing by Versa Press

Library of Congress Cataloging-in-Publication Data

Names: Kinsella, John, 1963– author.
Title: Insomnia : poems / John Kinsella.
Description: First American edition. | New York, NY :
W. W. Norton & Company, 2020.
Identifiers: LCCN 2020027340 | ISBN 9781324006473 (hardcover) |
ISBN 9781324006480 (epub)
Subjects: LCGFT: Poetry.
Classification: LCC PR9619.3.K55 I57 2020 | DDC 821/.914—dc23
LC record available at https://lccn.loc.gov/2020027340

W. W. Norton & Company, Inc., 500 Fifth Avenue, New York, N.Y. 10110
www.wwnorton.com

W. W. Norton & Company Ltd., 15 Carlisle Street, London W1D 3BS

1 2 3 4 5 6 7 8 9 0

for Don Paterson

Contents

Insomnia

The Bulldozer Poem

Bulldozers rend flesh. Bulldozers make devils
of good people. Bulldozers are compelled to do
as they are told. Bulldozers grimace when they

tear the earth's skin — from earth they came.
Bulldozers are made by people who *also* want new
mobile phones to play games on, *and* to feed families.

Bulldozers are observers of phenomena — decisions
are taken out of their hands. They are full of perceptions.
They will hear our pleas and struggle against their masters.

Bulldozers slice & dice, bulldozers tenderise, bulldozers
reshape the sandpit, make *grrrriiing* noises, kids' motorskills.
Bulldozers slice the snake in half so it chases its own tail,

writing in front of its face. Bulldozers are vigorous
percussionists, sounding the snap and boom of hollows
caving in, feathers of the cockatoos a whisper in the roar.

Bulldozers deny the existence of Aether, though they know
deep down in their pistons, deep in their levers, that all
is spheres and heavens and voices of ancestors worry

at their peace. Bulldozers recognise final causes, and embrace
outcomes that put them out of work. There's always more
scrub to delete, surely . . . surely? O *continuous tracked tractor,*

O *S* and *U* blades, each to his orders, his skillset. Communal
as D9 Dozers (whose buckets uplift to asteroids waiting
to be quarried). O bulldozer! your history! O those Holt tractors

working the paddocks, O the first slow tanks crushing
the battlefield. The interconnectedness of Being. Philosopher!
O your Makers — Cummings and Caterpillar — O great *Cat*

we grew up in their thrall whether we knew it or not — playing
sports where the woodlands grew, where you rode in after
the great trees had been removed. You innovate and flatten.

We must know your worldliness — working with companies
to make a world of endless horizons. It's a team effort, excoriating
an eco-system. Not even you can tackle an old-growth tall tree alone.

But we know your power, your pedigree, your sheer bloody
mindedness. Sorry, forgive us, we should keep this civil, O dozer!
In you is a cosmology — we have yelled the names of bandicoots

and possums, of kangaroos and echidnas, of honeyeaters
and the day-sleeping tawny frogmouth you kill in its silence.
And now we stand before you, supplicant and yet resistant,

asking you to hear us over your war-cry, over your work
ethic being played for all it's worth. Hear us, hear *me* —
don't laugh at our bathos, take us seriously, forgive

our inarticulateness, our scrabbling for words as you crush
us, the world as we know it, the hands that fed you, that made you.
Listen not to those officials who have taken advantage

of their position, who have turned their offices to hate
the world and smile, kissing the tiny hands of babies
that you can barely hear as your engines roar with power.

But you don't see the exquisite colour of the world, bulldozer —
green is your irritant. We understand, bulldozer, we do —
it is fear that compels you, rippling through eternity,
        embracing the inorganics of modernity.

MILKING THE TIGER SNAKE

Fangs through a balloon, an orange balloon
stretched over a jam-jar mouth scrubbed-up
bush standard — fangs dripping what looks
like semen which is venom, one of the most
deadly, down grooves and *splish splash*
onto the lens of the distorting glass-bottom
boat we look up into, head of tiger
snake pressed flat with the bushman's
thumb — his scungy hat that did Vietnam,
a bandolier across his matted chest
chocked with cartridges — pistoleer
who takes out ferals with secretive
patriotic agendas. And we kids watch
him draw the head of the fierce snake,
its black body striped yellow. 'It will rear
up like a cobra if cornered, and attack,
attack!' he stresses as another couple
of droplets form and plummet. And when
we say, 'Mum joked *leave them alone
and they'll go home,*' he retorts, 'Typical
bloody woman — first to moan if she's bit,
first to want a taste of the anti-venom
that comes of my rooting these black
bastards out, milking them dry — down
to the last drop.' Tiger snake's eyes
peer out crazily targeting the neck
of the old coot with his dirty mouth,

its nicotine garland. He from whom
we learn, who shows us porno
and tells us what's what. Or tiger snake
out of the wetlands, whip-cracked
by the whip of itself until its back is broke.

SEA LION

Where I stood on the rocks in front of the train workshops
there's a marina and the growth urge of the Midwest middle class.
Large boats with sport-fishing ambitions sit in their pens — wine
and beer are quaffed amidships. Ladies with headphones and prams
jog along the boardwalk. Inside the maze of channels green water.

Where I stood on the rocks in front of the train workshops
huge chunks of inland stone ward off the Indian Ocean. Builders
will tolerate no wrecks of pleasure craft within their remit.
But near the jetty not locked-off from non-subscribers
Tim spots a sea lion which bottles, dives, then emerges

alongside us — lolling, rolling, blowing stale air over green waters.
It dives under the jetty and we misjudge where it emerges
but it turns back and communes with us nonetheless.
I am guessing a sea lion would consider this 'relaxed', like us,
but maybe not because fish are on its agenda. But Tim is excited.

So close! How the leisurists feel looking out from their cabins,
or down from luxury flats overlooking their pride and joys,
is another matter. What does it mean, this reclaiming of land,
this enveloping of sea, the narrow opening to a shipwreck coast?
Three and a half decades have passed. I feel no nostalgia, only grief.

Where I stood on the rocks in front of the train workshops
I fretted about the sheds and machinery behind me, the shored-
up defences against rough seas, and opening to the right looking

out to the islands, the crescent of beach where in the shallows
I trod on a cobbler and knew blue murder was a toxin in the blood.

Where I stood on the rocks in front of the train workshops
I should have guessed what would come — the agonising expanse
of God and science, the juxtaposition of machines and the sea, the
    inevitability
of pushing out — nodules on the island continent, forces for and against
isolation. We stayed as long as we could, watching the sea lion.

SHARK TALE PARADOX

for those lost to sharks, and for sharks themselves

My grandfather kept small sharks in his saltwater tank
and I gazed up at them, mesmerised, wanted to see out
with their eyes. A Grey Nurse in a public aquarium

turned me to the sea from the inland of fear,
and I knew open water made its own histories.
Sharks became synonymous with liberty:

I saw them in the wheatcrops, in the rivers,
and staring out at sea when we reached the coast.
And later, in Geraldton, I skindived between them.

I saw White Pointers with jaws as wide apart as planets.
I know now I struggled with the 'God-shaped hole
in the human heart', whales tethered and at their mercy.

I heard a 'Bronze Whaler' was swimming the Swan
and Canning Rivers, and I was hauled out of the water,
standing sentinel on Deep Water Point Jetty, hoping to witness.

I saw a Shovel-nosed 'Shark' dry-panting on the wooden planks
of Busselton jetty, knife wounds in its body, teenagers poking
fingers into its mouth; 'deep sea' fishing, great white hunters.

Somewhere, I saw a Port Jackson shark marooned on a beach,
heavy hook still piercing its mouth like jewellery, the night
fading fast in its dulled eyes though darkness spilling out.

I saw a Wobbegong almost camouflaged among the reefs
of Drummond's Cove, and I watched it write Ss in weed and sand,
a script I knew I'd have to learn for making sense of the sea,

even the shallows which I swam, straitjacketed in wetsuit,
mask, flippers, snorkel, and weights to take me down.
I kept my distance, seeing fragments of its language.

I heard someone lost their toe to a Wobbegong on the same reef,
treading close. I don't think anyone demanded it be killed.
I could be wrong. I don't think there was a trial. I know

its case wasn't heard, a jury selected from its peers.
I have seen drowned sharks caught in nets, I have seen
them sliced open and hanging, insides out. Goaded from cages.

I hear of a resident Tiger Shark in Hell's Gates. The surfing
around it, but always alert. My brother has surfed the coast
off Geraldton for decades and says he doesn't know a surfer

who wants sharks culled. Surfers share the sea, know the risks.
I read of 'catch and kill' like a wanted poster from the Old West.
I read of 'baited drum lines' like a dragnet to convince the public

something is being done, that pain of loss to shark 'attack'
will be somehow lessened, if not overcome. But loss will only
bring life if it grows awareness; death sentences only diminish us.

HYMN FOR GIANT CREEPER SNAILS
AND THEIR SHELLS

Campanile symbolicum!

In the abstract, molluscs creep across the sandy seafloor,
en-shelled, dragging towers, owner-builders, grazing,
to perish and become rock-record in layers, cross-section
we marvel at in sediment anatomy eroded to reveal,
at Point Peron, rough seas and mushroom rocks,

while way out, deep-sea divers pillage other species
for their shells, plucked from *in-situs*®: a sales gimmick
built over life's nostalgia: as children, we pierce the marine
in wonder and later *re-collect* it to boost profits,
spiralling out of control. Spine-chilling.

Thus, Bell Clapper, slow uvula's
toll, not exactly 'going like the clappers,' slides
below a snorkeller's excited vision,
bells to chime in a wedding or funeral,
bells struck for hollow victories;

a collector's urge that's far from collectivist,
a resonance plucked from the water, Narcissus-
divers caught in rings of their own making observe
the turreted, the whorled, the cord of a concave spiral
left at neap tide, gentle waves stroking its apex,

a gambit of cladistics playing up the keel-
hauled ecology of conquest, exploiting
these 'living fossils' *dead or alive* through a politics
of exclusion, tangenting and making ad-hoc,
riding the coat-tails of 'keep them in their places'

self-preservation, this greedy exit-strategy.
To collect the *relict* — the chalk-white
abandonment, the green slime that illustrated
its aquatic face to the elements — washed off
as we churn in our childhood enquiries:

for me, along southern shores, reefs,
for me, imagining Giant Creepers
        haunting all depths.

SWIMMING POOL

for Lorraine and Tony

Not an expression of wealth but one of quiet desperation,
the heat and dry eviscerating hope — a giant shadehouse
of green cloth, and an above-ground keyhole
swimming pool, with avocadoes and ferns edging
the cement slabs, aura in the midday twilight.

And the red dust, too fine to shut out, decorating
the aqua-emerald waters, a wound open from an attack
of the inland leviathan, invisible as the filter strains
to remove impurities, leave pure as chlorinated amniotics,
and the dry birds squawking to be let in — *shriek-caw-shriek.*

Inland pool that was no waterhole, gnamma parody
down from the salmon gums and wandoos and pepper trees,
looking out over the sheep paddocks, the pig yards,
down onto the rat-tunnelled horse dam, out beyond the white-
walled house-dam of fated sailings, edge of the earth.

And this was in the Seventies, long before the rise
of pools on cocky properties, a nod towards a strong
swimmer, towards a childhood visiting the coast, a father
who loved the ocean. But there was a mother too, one
of the goldfields women who never learnt to swim.

Wheatbelt swimmers, wheatbelt pathfinders,
wheatbelt paradoxes carted in on the truck in riveted
steel cubes, brimming from standpipe flow; and then lesser
but regular cartings for 'topping-up'. Record the volume,
pay up later. And all those kids travelling from far

afield, travelling to take a dip, frolic beneath the shadecloth
cathedral, bathe in the gothic font of swimming pool —
Australian crawl, breaststroke, frog-kick where the sun
denies the existence of amphibians, and dirt looks past
the sky for an opening through which rain might fall.

BAT! IN TÜBINGEN, LATE WINTER

I have been watching a bat working the inside
of a right-angled triangle of buildings just outside
this window. Dusk is slow coming on and the bat
is sharp and slow-quick and induces a compulsion
to mimic. I read that no bats ever really get entangled
in hair, that this is pure folklore. But I have seen
it happen in childhood. Witness. The squeaking I hear
is really a chirp chirp bat hears and overhears
as it takes three storeys of the building I am
encased in, rides the insect columns up up
up then drops to skim over the top of the thin
and shallow but fast Ammer River. Skim is not
a truly accurate description of its movement
which is terse, jerky, but fluid. I am fixated.
Writing and watching at once. Caught up.
Entangled. This is no self-projection, and this
is no description. Snub-body is airborne
of exquisite ragged wings. I am not becoming bat
and I don't wish anything else on it. I am not
the bat on the stick from the showbag, one
of eight my father gave us each on an access
visit, an outing to the Royal Show, 1975. But
I loved that rubber bat, bouncing in front
of my mother, my brother. My father
never saw it. Bat is small by my measure
but a giant to insects, overwhelmed I must
state the obvious, reiterate. Precise and close

to the glass like ethics. The window
is partially open. It is winter. Late winter.
Bat is not from the cellar of the castle
but maybe from the patchy woods near-
by. Telephone repeaters work the invisible.
I am vulnerable to the signals, the crackle I think.
A slow-down, a flutter, my arrhythmia
to offset dying light. Mammalian flower,
take this down as a rant and ramble,
Hölderlin in Zimmer's tower,
making it his own, seasonal adjustment,
SAD, listen listen! Bat is not performing
as it's supposed to? It is at the glass.
It taps. I am not even suggesting a code.
They don't do that. They don't. Never never never!
Years and years in caves and I've never seen
it happen, says the researcher. Never ever ever!
Well, be here, be here, eye to eye, now. So close.
Body warmth. Cold hardening, viscous
to force on through. Wings mirroring
insects suddenly alight from within.

WAGENBURG

for Russell and the commune

I am listening and seeing and making
a picture of a place through a single trek —
someone's daily routine, daily encounters,

synthesised through conversation
and vicarious participation, but nonetheless,
I am there, walking and listening and seeing.

Past the only 'legal' hippy commune on public land
in Germany — Wagenburg, the fortresses of refusal,
of declining what's on offer in 'townlife', on the edge of forest

with trees marked with blue spots or slashed
with orange, separating the 'mature' from the rings
of witness to make the grade, selective logging.

But the barefoot kids of the Wagenburg know
the trees must *all* stand to make the light and shade
work the way it does, their palisades against regulation.

This gateway that is not a barrier. Nor is the gateway
of the old French barracks of occupation below, two concrete
pillars all might pass through without hesitation,

warzone colonised by civilians, friends living between
recycled barracks, looking out onto the forest,
up past the Panzer workshop, the Wagenburg.

As we walk higher, past a meadow sloping
down to the treeline, a warning: *down there*
is bad karma, it's where they shot deserters.

We won't go there. I will never go there.
But the people of Wagenburg offer hope
that ghosts have somewhere to shelter,
to wander in barefoot, be welcomed.

Searching for the Tübingen Friedenseiche (Peace Oak)

'The tree has been planted in 1871 after the war
between Germany and France as a symbol for peace.'

Oak tree memorial to the end of war
that served the newly laid-down empire
well, though who's pulling straws

when peace is at stake, the sapling
rising to make acorns for Eurasian jay,
who will stockpile like there's no

tomorrow, only a winter that stretches
time, or a summer that might incinerate
if you don't shelter under spreading

leaves. I want to find this peace oak
without the GPS scavengers use
to collect points, to encompass

the memorials to conflict,
dead strewn on a battlefield
bigger even than Zola. But

I can't find my way through
the strips of lush vegetation
hiding houses and roads,

enclaves of middle-class
virtue in a locally peaceful world.
But the oak is *tree* in its own right

and its one hundred and forty-six years
of providing for tree creepers and jays,
insects and songbirds, a wayside

marker for the collectors of data,
is massive in its soothing effects:
the oxygen it makes, the carbon

it eats, the haunting of a stark
sky when the tree's leaves fertilise itself,
the compulsion to find the peace
outside such 'politics', such history.

MUTE SWANS OVER CARRAIGLEA

Four with their white wings
'wheezing' a refrain, following
the black coastline. All life
lifts to their passing.

Seeing them is not dependent
on eyesight, sensing their musical
flight not dependent on hearing.
Each wingsweep bridges silence.

The leader flies higher and the others
stack below to step down so the first
is last, the second, third.
Harmonics are also involved.

All life knows this more than
its own sentience. All inanimate
presence shudders under the force.
Rocks shimmer, Carraiglea shudders.

SWAN CHEVRONS

Mute swan at a rapid rate
of knots sails towards the source
of the Lee, slicing up through
Ballingeary, splits the flow
and hooks us with its balance,
its avant-garde conviction,
an equidistant piercing
of greenery, severe white
reflection eating into
future's violent images.
Passing rapidly, but more
than glimpse, brings on that hunger
for answers: chevrons from its
passage, permanent anchors,
brackets and braces fixed to
banks, though flexible enough
to rise or drop with levels —
the steel of clock-springs, the steel
of floating bridges flouting
gravity, though this bridge we
cross is rubble limestone, arched
firmly against swans and flow.

POST-TRAUMATIC

For days, I've been watching
the lemon-scented gums,
Australian eucalypts, swaying
through gales in the garden
of Rose Cottage next door.

They have created a vicarious
connection with 'home'.
They are known as 'widow-makers' —
a propensity for dropping
limbs on spouses. Anyway,

I am feeling violently ill
because a bloke is chainsawing
the large 'specimen' in the back garden
down to the bone. Gums
and chainsaws. And the first

fine — crystal-clear — day
in weeks. The chewing at limbs
is the smell of southern summers —
the warnings, the bloodletting.
My spouse, Tracy, says, 'When

I heard that noise I knew
you'd have to write it out
of your system.' The lemon-
scented gum to be burnt
to ash with coal and peat.

GREY HERON IS NOT A HOOD ORNAMENT

The twelve-footer outboards in from the bay,
its ingress watched by gulls and the odd jogger.
The sea's a glasstop, so the chevrons from the boat's
passage tamp the harbour's walls. On its prow,
a grey heron, still as sculpture, staring down
the man tillering the motor. His haul under
wraps. The heron is in fully retracted mode,
compact and warping definitions of grace.
Its lack of animation prompts inanimate
comparisons: it looks more like a hood
ornament than a mascot. Patience
is another variable, with grey heron's
'stabbing' beak, its quick-as-a-flash
reflexes. All that immanence. A binary
relationship, a symbiosis, pragmatism
of hunger and symbols; whatever
works in the conditions. When the sea
is rough, such ornaments don't stick,
or don't try. The bird flies, though it will
come back if it lives another tide. One day
it just won't arrive, though another might,
enraptured by a semiotics of balance,
the stern riding low and unctuous,
a bellyful, a prow to be held in place.

Fingerprints Lacking in Bantry

To register a presence, the ancestral
fingerprint irrelevant to the Garda,
you place a finger on the glass
glowing red, blood offering,
and the officer says try again,
roll your finger, take some natural
oil from behind your ear and press
on the glass again, roll your finger.
And still no print will show.
Decades ago your prints were taken
in ink when there was still enough
of you to show, confirm
what they didn't want.
Have you worked with chemicals?
Laboured on a farm or in a factory?
That will do it, she says. I've seen
prints of a bookish man of seventy
that are so beautifully preserved
he could still be a child. But yours
aren't even a shadow of what you were,
burnt off and never coming back.
Great storms a fortnight ago
threw waves and seaweed
up into the Garda station,
picked away at the seawall.
The tidal surge that will
reach to the bay's elbow,

main town of the region.
Mountains hold it in place,
but denuded of their copper souls,
they too have lost their prints.
And the old forests have gone.
Little is left of the stretches of oaks.
And I have these blank fingers,
these shiny hands, made
of the emptying out, the tendency
to go elsewhere and wear
new worlds to the bone.
We'll deal with this situation
at the next stage, she says,
when residency wants
more than prints,
when you'll pay.

ORANGE 1962 MASSEY FERGUSON TRACTOR, CORTHNA, IRELAND, 2013

I know that tractor. I have driven a blue version
many times in the Avon Valley. Not as hilly as here,
but in the wet it gets boggy, and hard work
was its catchcry. Built the same year I was built,
it required less gestation time. I was birthed
early in sixty-three, probably around the same time
it arrived at Fremantle Harbour.

This one belongs to the landlady's father,
eighty-two and insisting 'she' will see
him out. The life they've shared together,
not mutually exclusive, but room
in the family unit. Almost a sisterly
affection, but not quite. It might be Mother,
but that place is filled eternally.

Machine grows into personality
but it's no case of a dog and its master.
Out into the fields of Corthna
it sucks in the Atlantic fogs:
factory and farm, longevity,
and maybe if the lid on the exhaust
breaks off, I can suggest a jam tin
wired over to keep rain out,
let the exhaust free into the idyll.

Pastoral Pointillism at Tim Healy Pass

At the high point of the famine road
cutting through the Caha Mountains,
where the white Mater Dolorosa thrives
over the slate architecture, the white
of sheep dotted against its transcendent
vision, raddled red heads, raddled
blue rumps, the hybrid red-blue sheep
flashing across the narrow, winding road
to blur the picture into focus. It takes
your breath away and fills your lungs
as clean as they're going to be filled.
In that paradox art is made and has
purpose, but not above all else.
The sheep as quaint as any pastoral
would have them, destined to serve
masters they barely know, following
their brethren from apogee to nadir.

SNAKES IN IRELAND

I am writing snake poems
in Ireland. The snakes are out
and hungry back home. My
ancestors came from snake-
lessness to watch brethren
die from toxins that defy
even imaginations that spoke
The Táin. Tracy says, You
had to come here to do that.
Tim says, A boy at school
said there are no mosquitoes
in Ireland and I replied,
Well, there might be a few . . .
To which he replied, There
are certainly no snakes —
everyone knows St Patrick
drove them out. Into the sea.
Into dreams. Into thin air.
The snakes I write — gwarder,
mulga, dugite, death adder,
king brown and tiger snake —
weren't driven to their haunts
by St Patrick. It was too cold
back then. But St Patrick is here
in the warmer days, arms open.

STITCHES

The tug when stitches
are removed is more
a reminder of mortality
than the excision and stitching
were themselves. That nick nick
as you hold the blue examination
table, half enjoying the sensation
because the middle suture
has become inflamed,
body rejecting it outright,
as it did the sun-growth
burrowing into your back.
To pass the time, quick
as the doctor is, you ask
the nurse assisting
how it went with the cows
on her farm, bulging with milk
after the storm knocked
power out. It's not rural
chit-chat — you are seriously
disturbed by the labour
cows are put to, you deny
the glory of red or blue cows,
the names of passes cut through
red sandstone amounting to victory,
the accumulation of ear tags
in the boggy patina of 'farms'.

Rather, it's an interest in pain,
the ethical underpinning
of our condition. Earlier,
when the lesion was being cut out,
the nurse was telling you
of her worry about the pain
the cows were experiencing,
having missed one milking.
You were finding common
ground in all your difference,
both of you in situations of reliance.
How you respond to the work
she does on your body, part
of her history, as the signature
of stitches plays with the script
of a scar to come. She'd told you
then that they'd luckily bought
a generator at a sale the week before
and were wiring it up that evening
to power the machines that suck
the teats, drain the udders.
You'd heard cows through the district
bellowing after the storm, the pain
of withholding, the memory of calves
long gone but clinging on. Too many
to milk by hand, just a favourite
relieved of her burden, and the confusion
of bulls in their distant *gort*. Cows
held in sheds, in stalls, bellowing
white blood with no heart

to recycle it. Just the drying out
that follows like deliverance.
Not the happy cows of Ireland's
dairy adverts, of its meat industry.
You weave veins and arteries
of ancestral irony, your forebears
clearing great tuart and karri trees,
jarrah and blackbutt, dappled cows
on grass itching on strange soil,
inflamed stitches. So you ask now
how it went, nick nick, and she says
that the generator was a dud,
didn't kick over once, and the cows
bellowed birth and mastitis and death.
But, she added as she stepped back
from the clean dressing, we hooked
up a wreck of a generator,
forty years old, that our neighbour,
an old German who can make
anything work — if it's broke
he can fix it — got going,
the machines relieving
the cows. A battle won.
Briefly, you thought of her,
that nurse, kind woman
with skill in her hands,
as Medb. Why? You'd been
reading *The Táin*, over and over
and searching for a clue in the local,
though set at almost the opposite

side of the country, a rewriting
of geography and patrimony
and hero-violence-epic language
cult, a release from *bondage*
in the southwest, the anglicised
namings, the residues of lingual
resistance, the Schulls, the overlays
of Marys and 'taking the soup'
ultimatums, as memory transcribes
into your Australian southwest
where small farms
under English landlords
buttered American whaling
ships, as you head back down
Ardmanagh, unravel the high place,
look across as the solid, robust convent
house, the religion your great-grandfather
and great-grandmother would fight over,
he taking to the forests with the son
he went to war with,
she staying with the youngest
and remaking them as Protestants.
You don't hear any of the labels.
In your secular isolation you
hear the cows bellow, yelling
across the district, a red bull
as large as the convent
battering its way through
Mount Gabriel, the white cupolas
with their hidden radars smug

in the misty rain, the red bull
with copper-tipped horns
smashing down Ardmanagh Road,
a truck laden with supplies
still trickling in after the great storms —
Christine and Darwin —
and as you throw your hands
up to protect your eyes
from the light, the sharp light,
you feel the deep stitches,
the hidden stitches
that will dissolve
into your body,
tearing away,
and white blood
lymphing its way
onto the dressing,
the milk of your settlement,
the ink of your residency,
you pacifist warrior
and freedom fighter for cows,
wondering at the ingenuity
of the old German, the rain
and the wind, the premonition
of storms from the Atlantic
'conveyor belt', the thin black shirt
lashing against you — no blue cloak,
no gift from your patrons —
and the damp dressing
covering your wound,

Medb heading home to her cows,
the doctor seeing his next patient
without prejudice, without fear
or favour, acclimatised
to carnage and peace.

SPRING TURNOUT

The fog clung on all morning.
It lifted and the sun made new angles
on the red sandstone of Gabriel.
Searching for different angles,
I discover shadow and copper
are patches welling up from inside.
Walks are like breaking the pentameter:
the repetition is never the same,
and the seven and a half million
trees down from Storm Darwin
shatter *sameness*: a delusion
of artists striving to be original.
My grandfather, a signwriter,
a 'master drawer' and oil painter
who hoodwinked modernism
for a few days, Picasso
in the closet, painted
the mill at West Murray
south of Perth before development
entirely rewrote *surroundings*,
sabotaged vegetation, questioned
the river's slow action. He painted
in watercolours from every angle
the conical building allowed,
and he painted from the same
angle to show the most minute
difference. Monet's haystacks

resonate, though I doubt he had
seen them at that stage. I say this
because the route of my walk
rarely varies, and yet change
is all that interests me. Friesian cows
have been released from two of four
sheds I pass — spring turnout
has begun. I heard the tearing
of grass from behind a hedge,
then cow on cow wrestling
with patches of green, blue,
brown, yellow, and the patterns
of their own skins. Some struggled
to position full udders, sitting,
half lying. Freer but confused.
They have their many ways
of saying absence of light,
but the sun is memory.
In the sheds where cows
are still trapped, I saw them
against the bars, catching sunlight
on their flanks, hinds, heads.
A desperate search for names.
A trauma over the dietary science
of silage, barley, straw, copper
and codeine boluses, the rigour
of originality in producing more
and more milk, the sameness of taste,
the discipline of 'bovine genetics'.
Regularity. Some look forward

to their summer drying-off, others
low over other breeds coming in:
Holstein . . . Norwegian Red.
The arterial highway, the milk
veins of domestication. I descend
towards town and down to the pier
where trucks are in to collect
the 'shellfish' prepared
and boxed, wrapped for market.
The hundred Carbery Isles
are misted-over, jealous
of their names, the tendency
of islanders to name favourite
birds bothering their 'fishery'.
This is the eclogue here,
stretched out, diasporic,
talking of family in Canada
and America and Australia.
My grandfather, Englishman
who arrived in Perth as a child
a few years before the 'Great' War,
would see his daughter married
to an Irishman's son's son's son.
Flour mills. Haystacks. Jersey cows.
Mount Gabriel's radar domes
('Gabriel's balls') stick out
like . . . familiarity, acclimatisation.
The radar waves wash over
locals and visitors, a technology
of the pentameter in the place

where seven-syllable lines
are red sandstone, and a woman
walks past with half a branch in her hand,
legacy of the great storm, and says
to reassure, 'an at-swim-two-birds
moment', Sweeney clinging
to the fallen tree, a nightmare
my brother will paint in the twenty-
first century, and I will think
of walking between cows,
listening hard for their names,
and the names they give
to each step of turf they cross.

FUNERAL ROAD

The coffins passed down the road
over boulders no horse could manage,
they knocked inside and out, cortege
from coast along spine of hills,
the only road, sou'-westerly driving
a Western Approach, as ground-
hugging furze scratched at heels.

Now it's the Celtic Sea that ends
just west at the Head, and an old sailor
whose mother lived on one of the Calves,
two families on a splinter of rock
balanced restively in the bay,
is cutting up pines forced down
during the storm. He calls to me:

I've landscaped this hillside for forty
years, and some time ago I uncovered
the *first* road, the only road west
of the harbour, stretching from village to coast.
It was known as the Funeral Road, and all
out here passed this way eventually.
Knocking inside and out. That storm

is spoken of in the same breath
as 1839's Night of the Big Wind;
so many ships wrecked. The *knock knock*.

And see here, the walls of an old house
on Funeral Road where all would stop
and maybe in famine find respite.
Bodies passed along the road.

Now sun in furze and the wind gathering.
I peer into undergrowth and see how
narrow the road was. It looks functional
in its own way. And mortared red stone
walls of the 'original house' built up dry,
a postscript to presence, the *knock knock*
of each slab added as buffer against the view.

The Old Ways and Swimming at Barleycove

'The weather is getting more intense everywhere in the world.'
Talk of the village.

Another orange alert. A big one coming in from the Atlantic.
We'll be red by tomorrow morning, interleaved with the storm.
Tracy has been stocking up with provisions, and while in the village,
she was told that 'the older generation' rarely, if ever, swam

at Barleycove; its long sweeping beach, the rock-walls projecting
deep into ocean. It'll be spring tide when the storm hits the west coast,
with dramatic surges inevitable — the coast eroded, town streets
flooded, seawalls undermined. At Barleycove the pontoon bridge

has already been removed, lest it be swept away into shipping lanes,
more garbage finding its way with the currents. Tracy is told how
before the pontoon, families bathing would get caught with the tide's
sudden influx, forced to carry picnic hampers back on their heads,

wading between sandbanks. Tomorrow, force ten gales will
leave their purple patch off the coast and lash plumes of coal smoke
vomiting from village chimneys. Tomorrow, heavy rain and sleet;
snow will gather violently on high ground, dust the radar domes.

According to the old ways of some, the beach at Barleycove is a death
-trap, swimming there a trick of the leisure class. At the bookends,
    where life-
savers lament summers, rips drag everything out, the bigger they come.

'If you're fool enough, swim only the centre, otherwise look on and
    wonder.'

Another orange alert. A big one coming in from the Atlantic.
We'll be red by tomorrow morning, interleaved with the storm.
Tracy has been stocking up with provisions, and gathering know-how
to make sense of what will come, traditions to read what's almost
    upon us.

Sizing Up Cape Clear Island with a Trigger Thumb

Out of the heavy quota of mist
the bevelled peaks of Cape Clear Island
demand you take reference: lock surveillance
from the sunny heights across Roaringwater.
So up high, you lift your thumb to take measurement,
to work proportions, how many heads of land
make a body length, how many heads above
sea-mist constitute the hidden island,
its lexicon of distance, its iceberg
beneath. It's not so cold here: Gulf Stream,
folklore, quadrupling of population and rents
in summer, legacy of mobilisation. Sizing up
the emergence, protrusion, floating islet,
you concentrate on your thumb, forget
what's blocked out, when it clicks down,
trigger thumb, ordnance action on the pacifist hand,
on the arm that bears no arms,
warped peace sign or Vulcan adieu amidst
prosperity. Thrown off by the odd angle,
the crowd's call, the big thumbs down
meaning thumbs up now, the translation all wrong,
mist seeming to reach over waters and up the ranges,
you don't recognise yourself. Hedges close in,
an ambush from ditches is possible, the lachrymose
cows you'd registered in their dead-shadowed shed,
staring into the sunlight over dozens of worn-out

tractor tyres. You snap your thumb back into place,
the bevelled peaks of Cape Clear Island
resolving to shape an image,
a knowledge from here
you can share with the islanders
over there, hidden in mist,
unable to see you unless
they've scaled the heights.

Elegy for a Kerry Highland Sheep
at Connor Pass

Over the edge of the carpark, stretched vista
to Brandon Bay, the wooden-posted ringlock fence
with single barbed-wire strand topping it like pride
of completion, the architectural monument
to enclosure, the compartmented mountainsides;
what emphasises is the lookout, the sightseer
epicentre, the epitome of pass — to the south-east,
Dingle Bay, and to the north-west the Atlantic
having its say against the strands wound out
to take the breakers, bog to sand, a roughneck
rousing of sublimity — postcard to the great
metropolises and their insularity. But what
interests and traumatises me — is — is the corpse
of a Kerry highland sheep clearly taken down
by Storm Darwin, deadliest storm since
the Night of the Big Wind in the early
nineteenth century, a corpse of straggled wool
and clots of flesh, the already eroded head,
skull protruding through, ill-shaped horns
twisted off by some force beyond weather,
legs trapped beneath the fence. Wrapped
on either side by mountains — Mt Brandon
with its teased snow, barely a cap, and Mt
Beenoskee, sending snow back up to steely
cloud, to ignore or pity, this residue of Darwin,
the evolutionary anomaly, battle for adaptation

against the bloody-minded fencing, resistance
to either side when legs slipping through
and breaking make a joke of separation.
The scratching around the unseemly body —
one fool in his people mover, having fed
the vulnerable family, gathered his rubbish
and hurled it over the edge, bypassing
the Kerry highland sheep corpse whose smell
was never lost to the howling, to the winds
too violent to be haunting, as in cars
it gathered, a sinking feeling, a dragging
down the narrow mountain road, the stench
of lowland fetor. But yes, the scratching
around the body tells me that another sheep
tried to prise the trapped sheep free: when
the winds allowed no visitors, when wool
braided and dreadlocked, horns hooking
the wire up without success, a moment
of mutual aid in the face of Lamarckian
bullying, those rubbish-throwers who
adopt his creed as precedent, unholy
howling on the precipice, so level-headed
in the levelled carpark, all falling to worry
beads, or prayers rubbed bare, those paternoster
lakes that catch the spirit which runs
in streams, cascades down the sandstone
jags and across dogged pasture, shapes
itself around the hoofs of sheep determined
to hang out, their slaughter in the eyes
of passers-by, the most enthusiastic

of their admirers, those to whom
'gorgeous' and 'authentic' come fast
to lips yelling into glorious view:
across the corpse or looking
the other way, pinching their noses.

RESURRECTION OF THE KERRY BOG PONIES

Grown out of bogs
ruffling manes over sods;
turf burnt in human homes
irritates their noses, smarts
their eyes: no love's
labour, just work
and its cost. To tread
hidden roads across
moss, black bog rush
and purple moorgrass,
following the lights?
No purity cult, just air
and rain and space;
shadows rising
from quasi-ground,
a quivering domain
toying with the sun.

CHAROLAIS

Tracy first saw this 'breed'
at the Nevers fair in Burgundy —
solid, low-slung bulls
she was slightly afraid of.

The neighbour here has been
separating his Charolais calves
from their Charolais mothers,
adjectives of (the town) Charolles.

In the exotica of flesh,
the genetics of French beef
are in demand. The shed
these Charolais are trapped in

is a boutique on the edge
of the village. A cow
knocks down a panel
blocking the window

and her head comes through
the concrete frame, searching
for the calf I saw being carted off —
she was lured back from a dash

into the field with a handful
of grain, but now she is calling
up an echo that rattles bones,
would add words to dictionaries

in all languages if we could
transcribe beyond howl,
bellow, wail, holler
bawl, yell or roar.

This 'separation' and her call
are an onomatopoeia
more precise than the church bell
which is less relentless.

CODA

They are a fair-coated cow
when out of sheds and under
the sun — green fields
igniting beneath their hooves.

HISS

At Lough Hyne parents rouse kids
to hiss but condemn the hissy-fit
when the order to cease
is ignored, all incited and in the grip.

Over-leaning a stone wall, stirring
a pair of mute swans to eloquence,
the combined hisses
trigger a localised squall —

an infectious hyperactivity
that makes an outing in 'nature'
an addictive spree, a confrontation
with beauty incarnate: the swans

disdainful of such mockery,
glaring back down their beaks
at parents whose cygnets
are floundering in the deep.

Wren's Electric Field Strength

Out of the furze and fuchsias
      to whisper sweet nothings,
wren pivots as fast and sharp
      as thought. With the domes
sending out high volts per metre charges,
      a house comes available.
Wren says, I'm resident year round,
      and will greet you here
on St Stephen's day. I won't die
      at your door, I will fly
below radar. And I say: I am not one
      for the old ways, and for
what it's worth, I'll watch out for you —
      nobody will put you
in a box, stick you on a beribboned
      holly branch, bury you
with a red cent. We never required
      Gothic in these parts,
says the Wren, the intricate vaulting
      of the hedges suffices,
and it always aspires up beyond
      the mountaintop. A gang
of boys passes by, striking hedges
      with hurleys, wary
of the girls walking ten steps behind.

HAY-BALING REALISATION OF SPACE OVER PLACE

'frequented place'
Michel de Certeau

At the 'high place' the fields have been cut dry
and baled as rectangles, their depth a story

I am familiar with. This is how I've cut & baled,
how growth has been put aside and preserved

in haysheds in the south of Western Australia.
I arrived, and stayed long enough to bale.

I passed through and admired handiwork
like my own, separating cause and event,

mice tunnelling through winter storage,
those 'little delinquents' in the farmers'

parlance. Mice know the best way
to go. But that's a long way away

in time . . . and space. Here, top of *Bothar
Ard Na Manach*, below Gabriel, it's unusual

to see rectangular bales over round bales
or silage set to stew into more than the sum

of its parts. And these bales are propped
upright into steeples, a 'wigwam' effect.

As a traveller I'd report straight back
to 'my' farming people, but I'm here

as much as anywhere, so I talk to Tracy
and talk to myself. I *could* send an email

through to Australia. Or write this poem
which operates on a time-delay switch,

letting the moment traverse each moment
of reading, the bales stacked on a trailer,

then shedded, doled out, eaten, converted
to flesh. And there's the politics of moving on,

of being moved on, shoved into the next
space. Animals and humans and silage.

Still, I give a nod to the boys compiling stability
(could be stable-fodder, but not necessarily),

labouring up at the high place, bales apace.

GRAPHOLOGY SYMPTOMATIC 4: FLORIBUNDA

Noongar calendar for now is the appearance
of moodjar blossom, orange/yellow with dry sunshine.

For the invaders, let's say, Christmas Tree. Maybe the few parleying
settlers of 1829 might have sensed a different cycle on those first

Christmases along the river and would have brightened
with its appearance, hemiparasitic, to drink the enriching fluids

of other trees. Seasonal decorations on farm gates, glitter and tinsel
in the headlights, sparklers in the tinder dry: armies of eyes.

Those searching haustoria of Nuytsia floribunda are like holidaymakers
and the Boxing Day lunch gathering at Wheatlands, year after year —

the networks of distance, the Avon Valley. Earlier today in Northam
I was swept up in the Christmas shopping avalanche, bare-handed,

weaving my way doggedly through wreaths of cigarette smoke,
the wheatbelt matter-of-fact *g'day, howareya . . . sorry, mate, it's okay*

exchange. Interlocutor, I wonder how little I write of the actual town,
this regional centre that's remained a constant across my lifetime.

Troubled centre of a compass. The moodjar blossom is growing
infrequent with the reclearing of the clearings, the double-dipping

into the zones. Still, their cables reach out under us, and I say
sorry and g'day walking past familiar strangers, concrete

beneath our feet and the last crops being harvested *out there*.

Graphology Mutation 25: the authenticity
of ploughing

Two old blokes — brothers — are working together
in the dry opening of winter to prepare their few paddocks
for seeding — a late seeding (they've got the timing right?)
alongside the creek just before it enters the river.

One brother is driving the tractor, an old Massey Ferguson,
without duals on the back and with a Robinson Crusoe umbrella
of piping and corrugated iron rigged over the seat — his *open-
to-the-elements* cabin — hauling a chisel plough which rips

into the topsoil but not too deep. The other brother is trudging
through the ploughed soil extracting dirt-encrusted roots
and branches that have fallen and been swallowed over
the time of its fallowing, have worked their way into the open

spaces like slime moulds, between animal and plant. These he
drops on a fire in its corona of ash, a liquid fire in this summery
winter light not quite right, a vacuole of damnation or resurrection.
He's not saying, and if he is, muttering under his breath, we're

not hearing. The field is ploughed weirdly as a rectangle, no curves
or roundings-out visible. The tractor's turns are 'impossible' right
    angles,
and the plough jumps to the guiding brother's incantations. Sounds
mysterious, but it's not. Force of habit, like their old shearing shed,

the spray pod that would hatch a triffid lusty with poison. And
in their overalls and peak-hats, they prepare to plant another
    season.
Last to plant, last to harvest. Small-scale but enough. Their silos
are cylinders without tops — a tarp will do. Authentic? Only those

outside the system would even wonder. Their neighbour Bob's
    operation
running a couple of 'STX 450 Quadtracs which pull 60' DBS bars
    with Bourgault bins' is about as real as it gets around here, and
    his operators
sit in exquisite cabs listening to Led Zeppelin as if they're setting
    roots.

GRAPHOLOGY SOULAPLEXUS 25: HOVER FLY

Over capeweed leaf, an arc 12 to 3, north to east,
precise — mimic, they say, they say, mimic

of wasp and bee, but maybe it's the other way.
There'd be a proof, but who would buy it

in this parcel of time, rejecting the science
we beg for in relative scarcity of knowledge?

From choice or from the hazy compulsion
of such rapid wings, my eyes 'capture'

and later my mind slows down enough
to see each wing stroke. The hairs of stalk,

dust on the leaf, an enthusiastic flower's
pollen brushed over its iris fixed basically

in place. Hover fly, some years you head
down to the city from the wheatbelt sun

when it warms all to a swelter, in such quanta
the media is full of panic. Ah, now, now

another hover fly has arrived 9 to 12 to 3.
Encompassing the stilled vertical—*over and above*!

GRAPHOLOGY ENDGAME 100: I AM A DICKHEAD

I am a dickhead in ways I thought I wasn't
I am a dickhead in ways people who call me a dickhead can't
    imagine
I am a dickhead in ways people who call me a dickhead can
    imagine
I am a dickhead with residues and hangovers of misapplications of
    beliefs
I am a dickhead whose interior was an adequate backdrop for
    exterior worlds
I am a dickhead who has tried to leap synaptic gaps to make
    conversation
I am a dickhead who in damning his past and his routes via
    heritage has liberated none
I am a dickhead despite the awareness of the dickhead moves that
    preluded me
I am a dickhead who has secretly thought *I am no dickhead* and
    that I am defying the paths of dickheadery I was injected with
    at school and by the state
I am a dickhead who lives and breathes the pollution I condemn
    and tries to hang on to life like my life is precious
I am a dickhead caught in anaphora because the mantra is
    preservation and conservation and forests still fall and bush is
    scraped back to bare bones
I am a dickhead whose epiphanies and self-doubts would liberate
    him from the damnation of exploitation and Western
    subjectivity

I am a dickhead for allowing the mining industry any leverage
over my life at all — I use implements manufactured using
their extractions, their abominations
I am a dickhead for not planting enough trees for using petroleum
products
I am a dickhead for deploying manners as a token of respect when
I sit uncomfortably in a roundtable confab, adding my two
cents' worth
I am a dickhead for utilising and being part of a monetary system
I despise
I am a dickhead for saying I need downtime like everyone else
— there's no time free and when I fall into the lush up-currents
of birdsong it is not enough to say I am *there*, nothing in the
absolute bliss of existence, as existence is so tenuous and the
deprivation of the right to a spiritual journey for *all* living
things nullifies the luxury of my own journey towards
enlightenment
I am a dickhead because I once thought sex was a natural process,
was more than a social construct, was a sharing on an equal
footing if there was consent, as if consent was chained by the
privilege of gender and identity
I am a dickhead because I don't think of my pacifist rage as a form
of violence, and caught in the paradox, critique each step I
take with motifs of calm to channel my anger
I am a dickhead because I am prepared to give up my life in an
effort to stop damage to other lives — peace at all costs, my
body crushed by machinery on the edge of a forest — trampled
down by the military, the constabulary, neo-Nazi Australian
patriots flying their Southern Crosses and Eureka Stockade

t-shirts, the Liberal Party, the Nationals, the right wing of the
Labor Party, and some of the 'left'
I am a dickhead thinking my words might make a difference and
the problem is not in the make but the kind of difference
words can bring because words can't be contained and
controlled and nor should they be, surely? Which leaves me
with what at the end of the day? as the tradies say as I co-opt
to my purpose.
I am a dickhead because I have so immersed myself in the
consequences of self and what constitutes the 'I', especially my
responsibility to my own subjectivity and the declaration that
for every action there is an equal and opposite reaction
platitude which I don't see as a platitude nor as just another
variation on self-mythologising which is an affirmation of
purpose when I too am nothing in the face of remorseless
entropy and eschatology
I am a dickhead who won't be held accountable when 'the
reckoning' comes, comrade*
I am a dickhead you might think is actually trying to call himself a
dickhead to avoid actually being called a dickhead or to say so
while believing he's not but I can assure you I know the truth
of it, and I *am* a dickhead
I am a dickhead who confronts people destroying the bush and
throwing a tantrum collapses as his heart falls out of sinus
rhythm and brings the world of nature he has constructed
down around his ears

* This is a reference to a communist marcher at a protest in Cambridge telling
me that if I didn't convert from anarchism to communism, my fate would be
decided at 'the reckoning'.

I am a dickhead who can't ward off the truth with a mantra as the
     bulldozers and heavy mining machinery are hauled slowly and
     steadily to the mines of the north with vast areas of bush
     falling to blade every day and the roadside vegetation
     vanishing despite a change of government as there's no halting
     the loathing and though there are many good people working
     to stop it, the hatred of life beyond self and family permeates
     this world this dickhead is part of this world this dickhead
     watches and dies a little more each day as he experiences and
     yet cannot stop the ravaging the rapacity the cruelty of
     'development' so what more can a dickhead do than declare
     himself than plead dickheadery?
I am a dickhead who talks too much in a place where 'lippy
     bastards' like me are held in contempt and I have the healed
     fractures of nose and skull, the cigarette burns and the
     psychological scars to evidence this fact though my saying so
     makes me more of a dickhead. Maybe you have to have lived
     here. Though that in itself is no proof as the hearsay, voting
     trends, main street of town, actions of land owners, and
     internet chatter will tell you
I am a dickhead who thinks he can in some *small* measure *co-exist*
     with the state he rejects when the state murders and robs and
     bullies every nanosecond of its existence while feigning
     innocence while claiming the higher moral ground while
     claiming it speaks with the approval of the majority
I am a dickhead who thinks the majority doesn't and shouldn't
     rule that only consensus has authority and a dickhead for
     whom authority is a lie anyway
I am a dickhead who thinks 'democracy' is about oppression of

minorities and not liberty for all — never has been never will never wanted to be

I am a dickhead who won't use pesticides or herbicides or fungicides but who lives in a realm where they rain down from neighbours and shires and farmers and contractors with the support and affirmation of multinational companies that are eating the earth to its core and claiming they make the world go around

I am a dickhead who doesn't think any job is better than no job. Not even worth explaining that — a condescension that makes me even more of a dickhead

I am a dickhead because school mates, teachers, police, government ministers, right-wing newspaper columnists, blokes in the pub, some friends and some exes, people yelling at me as I march and protest as I read poetry in public, tell me so. Oh, and some literary critics. Maybe more than some. I am not sure how that 'more than some' sits in the calibration of the personalised ('wank') of the dickhead scale

I am a dickhead because I am loved by my son and my partner and my mother and my brother and my mother's partner and my auntie and uncle and cousins and maybe a dozen friends. Which is not to say they might not privately think I can't be a bit of a dickhead on occasions but I am hoping against hope that they can cope with that and it's not simply out of politeness. What I appreciate is their tolerance of dickheads, and I'd like to think I've got a bit of that as well.

Graphology Endgame 101: IM Fay Zwicky

Fay's funeral is in half an hour and I can't be there —
I am deep in the country awaiting the delivery
of a load of drinking water: there have been bursts

of rain but it's a dry winter. When I spoke to Fay
on the phone for the last time, I think I mentioned
in passing the dryness, and now I think of those words

and I think of the dry and pall of smoke in her poems
of hospice care, her attempts at connection
with those who were closing off, or were hanging on,

or would or could only let fragments of others through
the doors of their lives. Fred, who thought her foreign!
Her humility and grace, her wry humour that told

me to keep on going in the face of negatives. Generous
moment that left me with something from a friendship
that had a long silence, decades of incidental encounter

but that had rhizomes in my childhood, through youth.
I told her as a young man as I walked past
that she was the most beautiful woman I had ever

encountered, went to her office when *Kaddish*
was published and told her it was the greatest poem
I had ever read. She invited my mother in as her student

to discuss Wordsworth, now part of our family myth.
All of this now, like the forgotten art of developing photos,
and her words on poetry, poet for whom being a poet

was an affirmation and mystery and a trial against
the bleak forces of the state and the callousness
of isms. In which reading was more than refuge,

it was liberation. But now, thinking over all this and over
Fay's poems written for friends who had passed away,
I am watching a pallid cuckoo following brown honeyeaters

whose nests when nesting time comes will be high
on its agenda for usurping, for egg-replacing, as
the fantailed cuckoos will deceive the splendid blue

fairy wrens that have moved here recently — entering
their dome-shaped nests, while their pallid relatives
go for cup nests. These are the details of my absence

from your funeral, Fay, the words that will see you
take leave of a contradictory world for ambiguities
you revealed in subtexts and allusions, those ancestors

you came to later, wondering over youth and ageing,
the nests we weave and the images we nurture
that don't always fit our desires, or troubled dreams,

or allusion or friendships that fade in and out of focus.
The cuckoos don't really fit with this, but they're
here, now, hanging around the edges of songbird activity.

I locate the descant, I pull out the stops, I listen to Bach
and Mozart. I say to a friend, one of your closest friends, that *I'll
be there in spirit*. And I am — the nests yet to be woven,

the eggs laid, and the cuckoo planning its entry
into the text of other lives. I have no place
in your afterlife as I had none in the earthly life

you left with humility and comprehension.
But your words of sharing and support,
your selflessness and irony,

your satirical edge with empathy,
are woven here for the future. And cuckoos —
you were not one and no conceit will make you one —

you knocked out no other poets' poems, and your
own did the work themselves, but with allusion
and portals through millennia of voices.

One of the fantailed cuckoos here
has had most of its tail feathers plucked
by a bird of prey — it sits close to the house,

its partner pursuing thornbills, making mental maps
for future reference. They are all about what will come —
and the damaged tail is accommodated in the prospectus.

And here, as you are sung, this offering of mixed metaphors —
soon the water will arrive and be transferred into the tank
on the upper tier, to be gravity-fed to the house, domesticity.

Disturbances in the Western Australian Wheatbelt

FORENSICS OF WHEATBELT SILO DESIGN

John takes Mum out to Frederik's farm
to see the olive groves he's tended for years —
a dozen seasons and she's never been there.

Afterwards, we receive photos
of their visit. Against harsh blue and sapped
yellow, open sky and dead pasture

fringed by stands of ghost-stricken
wandoo and native grass trees, the olive
trees push their Mediterranean mythology.

'He doesn't use pesticide,' Mum assures us,
a flagon of oil as parting gift and thankyou —
John has been a mainstay, a preserver

of the story, teller of the tale. Where wheat
and sheep had sway, olive trees warp
their way into the propaganda: 'produce

of the district'. But among the photos,
what really catches my eye is a unique
corrugated iron silo, silver but not lurid

in its setting, its concrete pad offsetting
the paddock's fall-away, steeply pitched
conical roof more than run-off, deflection of light,

steel-banded body like a corset. They still
give buildings and machinery female names
though the area is known for its innovations,

its revels in the pragmatic, its barnyard
philosophies with oomph. They subscribe
to a textuality of land and work, of labour

and practicality. The trick is in the opening,
the access point where grain is augered
or shovelled out — a metal rubbish bin

that's been lopped off at the base and inserted
into the silo's belly, a tight-fitting lid
suggesting control and craftsmanship.

I recognise this same craftsmanship
from Wheatlands farm, an innovation
of my uncle's, or at least 'in the manner

of' the district. It sticks fast because
it was a portal to the harvest in the middle
of winter: the auger inserted into its mouth

no warp in the business of the farm, our
swimming against the tide of grain, mice
levitating over the golden, pimpled skin,

the handfuls we scooped from the hourglass,
shovelling wheat or oats into sacks to feed
pigs and sheep, high on the volatile dust.

Needs must, I acquire more information:
it turns out Frederik's farm was once owned
by my uncle's best friend, a farmer-engineer.

The odd-looking silo was his design, and I hear
from my auntie that it was even stranger
than it now seems, having been built

with a mirror cone underground, a tapering
subterranean bowel, where grain was to be
sucked out by an auger when the above-ground

supply had been depleted. But the best-laid plans —
that country credo: an underground stream
collapsed and floated the structure, the silo

listing and sunk. Righted, it was concreted
flat, and the sub-cone reduced to a rusting
vestigial limb, a whisper on the borders

of story-telling, an underworld myth.
The portal access is its motif now, its rocket design
an upside-down compensation, a wheatbelt

axiom, a Socratic moment as the sheep
looked on bemused from their symposium,
with one or two 'ugly wethers' having

the foresight to know all things change,
a forensic moment that says from failure
profit will be made — an augury of olives.

I've yet to tell Mum how I pieced the jigsaw
together. Connected her life to John's, the land
to a restless history. It is said the oil

from those groves is of excellent quality —
many awards have been won and it's a boost
for the tourist industry which cares little

for stories lost, for stories retold, remade.

The Gate is Barred by Ants

After the downpour, hardground softens
and the red ants spread their colony

out under the drive, emerging
and thrusting cones of damp dirt

upwards — it's too easy to say,
'Like volcanoes', as they spew

tephra. We might add 'crazed'
and 'swarming' when they are not

the former, and the latter is a word
designed for propaganda. This region

where no active volcano has enacted
for millennia (on millennia), precision

as lost as British colonial generalisations,
the ants instigating their processes

across the gravel driveway the crossover
where we leave and re-enter this presence

but now are brought down by rapid responses
of red ants streaming over our feet up our legs,

biting hard and keeping us from making
our way. Whose rights and what subtexts

are brought into play? This structuralist
standoff, an awareness we're still hanging

around on the edges trying to find a way
through, wishing no ill but desiring the space,

to avoid their 'setting in' — look at us!
standing there, hopping mad but not angry,

just reacting to formic acid injections,
all similes and epithets, all idiom

and local experience. This opened gate,
this message to travel by another path.

But you can't read anything into it.
We take responsibility for our own acts,

our own use of language. This hotspot
not on geopolitical surveys, unwatched

by volcanologists — writing back to an authority
we don't recognise, we owe nothing to —

what we owe being to those whose place it was, is.
Is. Is. And the ants. Whose place it is also. Truth be told.

Crossing over, moving between points, the gate stuck
open or closed, no barrier to ants, to facts, to metaphors.

INTUITION

'synthesis of apprehension'
Kant, *Critique of Pure Reason*

I know I can hold it together.
Some who have not known me
in my sober life, in my years

at Jam Tree Gully and further
back, too, wouldn't believe
it possible. Can I go a day

without describing what I see
walking the slopes of the block,
looking out this window, all

mediated through the process
of reading and recording? Sure,
I can. But why would I want to?

Every moment *is* and *isn't*
empirical here — I am not speaking
for your zone of reading, those

embellishments of the world
as you see it, taking this in, too.
Apparently, the storms have

released a bacterium
from the soil — it is called
a 'deadly and ancient disease'

in news reports, having been
lifted or propelled or compelled
into the air, this tropical melioidosis

travelling far from the tropics,
as far afield as Toodyay, not far
from us. So walking out

is different from looking out.
We reprogramme perceptions,
experience knowledge. Space

and time and intuition
can so easily distract us.
Make us less attuned. To soil?

More vulnerable. But listen,
hear the bronzewings'
'nervous' love song —

bold and confident
to appropriate ears. Intuition.
And the spectre loose

in the air from the soil,
but chances so slim, rare.
Manifesting in 'livestock clusters'.

Clusters of animals restrained
by fences. Contained? Hear
their human representatives.

Listen, and don't get distracted
by the bronzewings' private song?
An overcast humid day, out there.

'BUZZ POLLINATION'

Yes, that's a blue-banded bee
making a burrow in the knuckle

of yellow sand that's been there almost a decade,
left over from house-building, set as rock.

This native bee is a solitary, but building
with an openness to other mothers-to-be

as neighbours — birthing rooms and cribs,
best address tenements, apartment block:

communal yet separate, a socialist utopia?
Quick in, quick out, to carve comfort

or security. And out and about, its feeding
zone — one in which pockets of pollen

are held back, kept in stock, selectively
available to those who can unlock

their puzzles boxes. Such vigorous,
vibrant winging in proximity, such grip,

such body action intense and stimulating;
this mutual aid of 'buzz pollination'

so many voyeurs rave on about. At home
now — nesting, digesting, laying.

Sheep Evenly Space Themselves

I've observed this before, even 'reported' it
in the hope people will realise what's at stake —

sheep deploying themselves across a paddock
evenly space — precise. They distribute

themselves, arrange themselves. I watch
and they graze turning on the points

they have selected, evenly spaced
gridwork — if the pasture is fairly

consistent, they have allotted themselves
no more or no less than their neighbours.

If aesthetics is at work, then people
holding sheep within fences,

and people who will slaughter them,
should contemplate this universe, fate?

You see, I have observed this before
and it's not a chance occurrence.

Would you call it a phenomenon?
Will you accept it as rhetoric or data?

As empiricism or lyricism?
Sheep evenly spacing themselves

in the paddock to the west of Toodyay
Road, just north of the dangerous T-junction

with Clackline Road. To the millimetre,
and compensating for thickness of wool.

Space Arc Space Ark

'Remove from your emptied concept of a Body everything
that stems from experience, one by one: colour, the hardness or
softness, the weight and even the impenetrability, and there still
remains the space which the body (now entirely vanished)
occupied, and this you cannot remove.'

Immanuel Kant, *Critique of Pure Reason* (intro, pt. II, p.4
Penguin edition trans Weiglet based on the Müller trans, 2007).

If I see the house as a boat
finding purchase on the valley wall,
and the remnant vegetation the damaged sea,
and the delta — vertical — on the curved tank wall
lapped by passerine birds, bobtails, black-headed monitors,
and describe how the kangaroos would come and patiently drink
damp gravity, then you might count my experience
as *inland sea legs*. I crave no acknowledgement
of being here, because I can't claim anything,
but it doesn't completely mean I am unwelcome — I cling
to this hope, on the hillside, draft keeling as storms
build at the festive time of year, as some call it, but not necessarily
me; edgy arc that sails towards no god, lacks an ark's gravitas,
strains in the heatwaves, expands and contracts against building
specifications, the caulking growing drier and powdery,
topsoil blown or washed away, and the threat of salty
incursions late in the piece. I touch the rainwater tank
to measure depth through concrete — differential between

water and air, sun on the round, the limey extrusion
where leaks dry as the freshwater ocean recedes.
This water we share with what remains here,
what floats thirst on the slope, weird river bank
failure in the dry, stepping off onto land that is dust.
This house, York gums masts bent and hollow,
jam tree sails, and a cabin that creaks with hope, *welcome*.

The Bonfire of Vanities Wheatbelt Style

The Corsinis let their artworks fly to the Antipodes,
so far from Florence. Savonarola's corpse
burning in the Piazza della Signoria.

He is burning on a cross alongside
a couple of mates. We are chockfull
with the carnival of burning:

raze precious objects (even
Botticelli pitches in), signifiers
and property of wealth/power,

and you too will be burnt, postscripted
by your own writings. Heresy
is such an easy *control* in games

of possession — like bonfires
illuminating this district, wheatbelt
firewatchers gathered around

as those most precious artworks —
bulldozed flooded gums, York gums,
even short-lived acacias, dried off

to the point of eruption even on cool
nights — are lit-up Toasty. And weather
warnings falling as extra silent ash

on the parade: *Don't burn*
before the front hits . . . high winds
are almost upon us, still as it is now,

the flames tangling with sky,
inciting stars that have been in hiding.
All of this to people champing

at the bit during the hot months,
fire held at bay (though cigarette
butts still flew out car windows

to touch a habitat, set it off,
heat of the sun), champing
at the bit for winter when fire

makes complete sense and nothing
will hold back, not even the monstrous
dry that has left all dehydrated, ready.

No one wants to remember the sparks
from a header striking a rock
during harvest bans. *Or or or.*

That was back then, this is now,
as if the calendar says it's fire time,
so fires outdoors will be had,

and mulled wine drunk,
and the watchtowers
switched on. *We are here!*

This ritual, this *rite de passage*,
this art lesson — *plein-air* is a night
habit here, as sparks fly

flyers burn, or whichever
insects are triggered from bark
by the igniters, the worshippers.

Borromini's Perspective and the Galleria Spada's Resident Cat

'The cat becomes a tiger in there, and the statue becomes so small.'
Valentina (at the front desk)

Seventy centimetres or thereabouts of Roman warrior
down the columns and arches to a vanishing point
all thirty-five metres we envisage as not much more
than eight, all those tricks of desire for more

than we can see, all those answers to immensity.
Green oranges brash as ripeness to come,
and bold cat full of God and Sun preening
a corner to soften the lines, make geometry

a choice, organically precise. I ask Valentina
if he wanders further than the chain which no
visitor can pass, and she ululates and insists
he becomes tiger while the statue diminishes —

that small warrior in all of us showing off,
law of the jungle, wildcat in its lair, focal point
of those empires we make from art, envisage
when enemy troops are at the city's gates.

ARMS AND THE MAN (ROME)

'Arma virumque cano'
Virgil

Breathing, tormented statue of Garibaldi
        on the brow of the Janiculum,
loads and fires his cannon of belonging,
ticking off the sun. A high point?
        We wonder demolition
or catastrophe in our unknowing,
a cloud of sulphur enveloping.
        We won't know why
for hours, though it should add up.
Bells strike and shimmer across the city.
        The beggars you give to
and the beggars you don't. Who sees whom.
Low rise against the decline of day,
        all the way to Sabine Farm.

EVIL COUNSELLORS AND OTHERS — FROM THE FIRST MOVEMENT OF LISZT'S 'A SYMPHONY TO DANTE'S *DIVINE COMEDY*'

The humanity! Degree in Western Civilisation,
progressive flames spilling from the chariot, and secrets
of fire squabbled over, citations mounting, Nation

a collator of dutiful deeds, useful knowledge, treats
to be distributed on the world stage. Cash for knowledge,
gift of the gab, God-particle funding arrangements (humanities!),
    feats

of otherworldly potential, a flaming waterfall driving a wedge
between conscience and hubris (such research will benefit
us all!), these deliberations of prayer, delivery systems, cutting-edge

research into why the path of destruction was inevitable — remit,
pay-off, *even* those *poor* ditch diggers will enjoy the run-on effect,
    the trickle
down; and see the political hacks welded into a *solitary flame*, hear
    them transmit

their frequent-flier meltdowns, Christian values precedents in
    Ancient Greek oracles,
museums of mining, entrepreneurial libations to baptise the ship of
    state,
nicknames Diomedes and Ulysses bandied about Canberra
    restaurants — coracles

on Lake Burley Griffin with its semi-stable water levels (see, see!),
    rate
signs of voter confidence in direct proportion to comfort of
    guardians of Western Culture,
energy security, gift of the gab, textual affirmation by Urkund,
    cut-rate fate.

ZOO (OR GULAG: A DEPARTURE FROM THE KHLEBNIKOV'S 'ZVERINES')

Search for Khlebnikov's 'Zoo' and you get his 'Zaum'
(Dedicated to G.S.)

O Gulag of Animals!

Where metal is the stalk of a sunflower and stars weep for the
micro-animals trawling the walkways for litter.

Where Coke and Wine are slurped up straws.

Where men duck away from their wives for a reconnoitre of the
ablutions.

Where birds mix feathers in the great aviary and raptors pick seed
from their neighbours' eyes.

Where the camel treks back into Central Australia knowing that as
so many generations have perished there, there can be no other
home.

Where electric fences challenge the deer to heraldry.

Where sports shoes emit light frequencies counter-indicative of
sleep.

Where gunfreaks imagine trophies and *bullseye!* the odd human
they wouldn't mind mounting.

Where black swans gather free at the ponds and raise a right red
fuss, hissing the length of their beaks, upsetting white
supremacists.

Where peacocks fuse light and sound and test the bounds of ego as
if the stage is a tentative surface not in the least like the texture
feathers were incubated out of. Fanning their colourful, fixated
eyes.

Where the lyre's mimic is the bird of the eastern forests: it barely
works as a nationalist symbol here out west, though we love the
thought of its intricate tail, its ability to imitate a football star
or soldier or chainsaw.

Where the roar of the footy crowd rumbles our eardrums, and the
sarcasm of Diggers means death is no further than an American
chopper will carry it.

Where people enjoy staring at the rear-ends of monkeys and
divining their (whose?) sexual fortunes. This form of bestiality
is encouraged. And monkeys make useful scientific test
subjects. All of a measure.

Where uranium companies with the footprint of an elephant on an
ant's nest — please, leave the animals out of these analogies —
build fables of love and tenderness and surfeit and generosity.
The older the land, the more administrators worship euthanasia.

Where bears have the gall to look like they're applauding their
    own performances, one eye on their keepers and the keys.
    Dressing up glee with an ambivalent look some might mistake
    for a dance of sadness.

Where flying foxes have already been deleted as a species though
    they still fly in the far north-east in search of fruit to whet their
    appetite.

Where the rare brown falcon works between developments and the
    storms of pillage that bother the hills with fire and smoke.

Where stubble-quail *quail* before thrashing headers, short sharp
    flights as the burn-off widens to become conflagration in rising
    temperatures.

Where the tiger is defanged against the window of the world and
    stalks its striped shadow, while inland a visiting Dutch racist of
    the so-called Freedom Party marches in the streets of the old
    wheat-town with his henchmen, billeted in bliss by those who
    tout his 'free speech' hatred as indictments against Muslims
    young and old. Let it be known my brother will marry a
    Muslim woman and that we shall be in attendance.

Where taxonomy is power and the state makes religion from desire.

Where the names of unnamed animals slip away before Data
    Central can capture their semantic essence for all magnetic time,
    flesh vanishing faster than the eye of a camera is able to
    capture.

Where animal voices are welded together in the plenitude of blast.

Where sea-lions bask in oil spilled from the ships fighting the
slaughter of whales.

Where dead souls of murdered blue whales and humpbacks and
sperm whales and southern right whales are marked by flags
which part the indelible inks of childhood from the page of
wonder.

O Gulag of animals, where the depressurising eyes of all creatures
bring into focus the text and images of visitors' brochures.

O Gulag.

Where an eagle watches its eyrie burn though it's the heart of
winter: those who fight fires to save us in summer make fire to
burn what's left in winter.

Where polar bears mark a category error through covering their
noses; in the green cement lagoon they eat fear; the Gulag sunk
deep into the membrane of the other, a plughole for history and
culture, for the literature of faraway places, even Siberia.

Where mountain goats climb the cemented rocks and look down on
unhappy and over-excited human children with disdain and
suspicion. Territory is at stake.

Where the giraffes lose muscle-tone in their necks and they become
as vulnerable as our way of seeing tells us; as if in confirmation.

Where the blast is the sound-barrier being broken outside of
standing orders: all birds equalising, and looking up as if
under water. Some have never swum before.

Where the greatest eagles are still seen as exceptions to the
'protected species' rule. Invoking the lamb, the hunter eats his
lamb sandwiches first, then shoots.

Where an eagle sees its talons hanging from a farm fence.

Where an eagle — massive — perches on the carcass of a dead
kangaroo, unwilling to move even when a Kenworth truck
— more massive — barrels down directly towards it and its
carrion.

Where a path takes you through pseudo-savannah, species from
all over sniffing rear-ends, trying to nut it out, make do. There's
no sign these herbivores are going to eat or fuck each other.
They're just wondering, sorting it out.

Where a deer nips your five-year-old pinkie through the bars.

Where the seal performs its own acts 'of significance' and is
suddenly made aware that it doubles as entertainment:
applauding his cartoon-self, he speaks up and stimulates the
funny juices. If this isn't generosity, what is?

Where the modern keeper has the little beast wishing he was its
mother.

Where sleepy assignations with zoo beauticians fail to keep the lion's mane from looking unkempt.

Where the clatter of horn and antler against the bars is enough to stir up trouble: remorseless!

Where God is a feathered friend, an ugly duckling, a webbed-footer in the desert, rain an irony they can do without. Dry as bones. It never happens.

Where guinea fowl are sentinels roosting in lower branches of tall, broad trees: incarcerated chickens listen out for the flutter, the first sign of the fox coming, or the drunken human with a sudden hunger for chook when stars are out.

Where there's slaughter of emus on the border, roos in paddocks, dingoes out on fences; where a gunman mowed down people in Port Arthur: a name that resonates in so many ways in so many places.

Where unpacked wolves wonder where to go next: up against it.

Where those entering the nocturnal house think they'll see everything: that weird light, the small enclosures, the sparse cover: it should all be there, available for the widening eye. But the nightbirds peer with wider eyes from on high. Adjust.

Where a walrus passes as Nietzsche's moustache: who gives thanks for songs, anecdotes, and sexism?

Where alpacas watch over flocks of sheep, warding off carnivorous ghosts without shape or denomination.

Where projection has the rhinoceros kitted-out in the armour of a tinpot tyrant, viewing himself in a mirror, wondering why extinction (outside himself) matters. But cooking the history books, he concludes an audience *is* necessary. But only one that claps as he preens himself. This has nothing to do with *rhinoceroses* or a *rhinoceros*.

Where seagulls hold right of way and snatch at their entitlements. There is no judgement here: just watch them catch the sea-breeze: we are driven over the sand dunes while they sweep back out over the waves.

Where totemics are a politics of belonging. And a spirituality. Who declares whom connects with what. To get to know one's quarry: becoming animal, if briefly. *But then* . . . also, where football teams are called The Falcons, The Eagles, The Seagulls, The Tigers, The Lions, The Kangaroos — it's a long list. They hunt each other down then lick their wounds or crow from the highest parapet to meet in combat again. Nation picks over carcasses. It's always hungry.

Where the duck's red beak hints that it has been dabbling in blood. We know this can't be true, unless it's been tending its own wounds: leadshot from hunters. Its nest grows cold.

Where elephants teeter in outback wildlife 'sanctuaries', blasted out of their homelands. After the poachers have ripped the

ivory away, they celebrate the glory of their AK47s (national
heroes, if ever there were ones. Or one. Eponymous). Elephants
are subtexts to the argument; their skins heaped high, bones
askew.

Where animal skin binds the codex: a hoax is as good as an
original: in the end it comes down to the language. The
language of animals and origins?

In creating this version or 'departure' from Velimir Khlebnikov's
'Zverines', I consulted the Paul Schmidt translated *Collected Works
of Velimir Khlebnikov* (Vol. III, Harvard University Press, 1997),
and sourced background information from a number of other
(scholarly) sources. However, it is its 'own' work.

RED

[with Liszt's 'Purgatorio' from *A Symphony to
Dante's Divine Comedy* playing in my head —
thinking over Cantos XV and XVI]

Red is sleep before the long fast dry has made red
of most things — a powdery bleeding, a sweeping
irritant flow. This great storm we rely on. Tirades.

What the smoke takes from us at the end is the lighting,
not the day. It gears up on waking, the shed leaves
of a dream of red — what will be written, enclosing

in the hours to come. Already the wind sheaves
its prepared piano — in lockdown, we know the timpani
of window in its frame, that might shatter the grooves.

It's where the music carries or drags across scenery,
across black & red, across a blue hope that dumps
the spectrum off the precipice. But the hills are leery

and squat — though edgy. Really, the red air thumps
the red shed, fusing with the ground it sits upon. All
is stirred up, the deluge striding behind the crump

of ploughs. Indoors is the only way — I test your recall
of red and my eyes seize up with grit, the red grit
of the contemporary. You'd expect the wrathful,

the percussion of their weapons lost in the howl. Shit-
stir. We won't know what hits us, what tears the corrugated
iron. Invisible fronts made visible are where the mythic

arises, not just out of earth or sky or night or day — bled
sunrise and sunset we won't collect in our memories.
If not waking to the loss of a reason behind the hand-

written red, what have we? Love takes a word, a series
of words, to find a way through the earthsmoke. Agnus Dei.
And yet there is no religion, no belief in the piano's

disruptions, as fluid as a greenhouse apartment — say
in New York, say as a composer recollects making wires
and hammers sing 'Mysterious Adventure'. Which way

will red take us as the year unwinds, the fires
of burners kicked up, unleashing? When will the deluge
change the story? I know you dreamt the red book, the spires

of text, the fonts of despair. This hunger, this rogue
aftertaste compelling more of the same — our supply
of experience. Look through the windows — a rouge

smear across the universe. Your favourite colour plies
the world with shades, with slight shifts — carmine,
scarlet, vermilion, crimson, dragon's blood where lies

the end of the spectrum as we know it, desire the warn-
ing, the lost in the distance . . . Who would ever describe this sin-
ful light as strawberry? Maybe an artificial dye — alizarin —

and where that takes us outside the zone's comfort
of your dream I love to hear, taking front and centre
then fading away. Remember, remember, it wasn't

in Rome we saw the two suns but at Ostia Antica,
on our way to the port, the way out we couldn't take,
the merchant ships having long sailed back to the outer

limits of their range, searching out red, speaking red — fake
value added to trade. But we saw the suns, and we went back
to the centre of the ancient city, to the ruins which forsake

any worth we might have to the people passing, a stack
of images compiling on memory chips we're sometimes
caught in. On? Warm days cold nights and a lack

of constant to calibrate by — reset. No, the storm
is almost here, and the fires whipped into the sky
lie about the nature of smoke. Our carbon forms

parodied by our accents, our recountings. Pack the esky
with perishables, check the torches — the power is sure
to go off. To go out into the red is far too risky.

Sleep will come eventually. Sheep make for shelter
that's not there — trees deleted, no alternative provided.
All small birds gathered together. We dream of colour —
of red and redness, wrapped around each other.

INSOMNIA

There were ants when I slept ants all over the gravel
and all over my feet. I do not have an antipathy

towards ants but they were electric climbing my legs
and I knew sleep could be no retreat — breaking

free into wakefulness I dropped the pronoun
and let the dark eat its fill. Dispersed and yet

hanging together as a cloud, swept out onto
the block, infusing wattle blooms equivocating

with cold and darkness, a bee out of synch
with the roll of the world. Locate 'me' in that?

Anathema of sleep. Restorer of consciousness
and bringer of mental health? Why the gunshots

then? Why the exponents of hunting assuming only electric
eyes — hot shot — if any protester/s be watching, and there

are ways of distracting and distorting the crosshaired
images? Owls are out (t)here, so full in tepid darkness

those hunters might worship them if they didn't
feel so threatened, so full metal jacket. What can sleep

do but block out hope of witness? To make pictures
of deathknells where silhouettes are, to complement

without extraction. Where is sleep in this, these portraits
of breaking twigs and the hush of nightwalking?

Keep an ear out, light peeled away from eyes,
the mish-mash of clichés and sensory deprivations.

I am back again, and I have never slept, not
really — not in the way other creatures tell me

they sleep. I will possess half the lifetime they'll have,
but as much time awake. *That* leaf is a 'hush leaf',

that one is a 'crackle' and *that* is 'whispering death',
and finally, 'a lift into the stars' — all of these

are easy to recognise if you retune to the tremor
of time always resetting, but never arriving. Crack

of the bullet. So, just what do powernaps do to ants —
meat ants/gravel ants? Trigger a hoodwink, a servicing

of their queen? Such family histories run-through fast
in the colony? And monitor reptiles murky with chill

closing fast, relatively speaking — how could I
disrespect their cold-blooded shut down? My blood

is without temperature, which I don't need telling
doesn't make me special. 'Your never sleeping

makes us feel uneasy!' Don't worry, I keep to rural spaces,
away, and acknowledge no coordinates are mine.

No longitude, no latitude, no intersecting lines. No points.
I was there at sowing I will be there at harvest, doing

my bit but surely no malign influence, however
the yield goes? Sleep is the subtext of religion,

which is how I know no real ants really emerged
from the hole in the palm or palmtree, no sugar on the tongue

of the filmmaker. I never trusted *Un Chien Andalou*
which I watched nineteen times in a row, same

number of times I watched *Blue Velvet*, in a row,
un-alone with desires. Ant farms of childhood

kept my eyes glued, the movement of eggs,
the hopes they represented. The precise shiftings

of sand. Even now, tackling orange gravel, a laterite
bonanza, the skill in pushing aside. What wheatbelt

life can be had outside the early hours of the morning
road accidents, the cataclysm of a car finding a lone

and ghost-lit tree in the long paddock? These commiserations,
the sack of the body a repository for incomings. Fallen

asleep at the wheel? Fatigue betwixt the crops — Gamenya, Kite
wheat, or GM canola: rude dust of dry seeding and its grim hopes?

Sleep is the only *ars poetica* you might wish me to write,
but I can't. No way. I've no skill no technique no style just wake-

fulness *out here*. And this? A signing-off, a resignation
to sleeplessness, an elegy, an ode, a hymn, an encomium.

A self-indulgence as rain finally arrives finally sweeps
in to lift the jags of salt crystals higher to the sun. And night.

It never began, the sleep; it never began. An early teacher
said, You've got ants in your pants. And the disturbance

set in. But that wasn't here, on the edge of the hills,
great wrecked open plains spreading away, burning edges

always chasing a centre that surveys can't locate. Follow
the ants, someone said, and I said, stark awake in the wee hours,

staring at the redshift-blueshift of the back of my eyelids — *I do.*
He's got a sense of humour, if you dig. That was said, too.

And: But how much expertise does s/he have in the matter
of sleep? It's just experience without years of training

to back it up. Leave sleep and sleeplessness to the experts.
In the repetition I found and find solace. Forage lines

stretching out — cartels of consequence. And, žzžzżing
of the tractor tapering the valley in ground-down powdered

soil statements of occupation — the adenoids jerking us back
into waking when sleep finally comes on. And loud gossip

night or day churning through the valley booming over onto plain
is a worry. Someone has been listening and watching

and wanting you to know they'll act against your state
of (in)difference — theorising of the non-normative

theorising the ants away when they slept and I didn't for they
don't have ants because they spread ant-killer and on larger

'infestations' they strap elongated packs to their backs
and go for a wander to paddock gates and let loose. Phew!

So, it's the movement of antennae, the collective
intelligence of ants working the angles

that necessitates my staying awake.
In awe I try to tune in — fluttering

my eyes (or your eyes) in rapid movement
I send back snippets of this life anti-life.

Some people might call it betrayal.
Some ants might watch movies

all through the night, merge sunset
and sunrise, ground and sky.

Emily Brontë Storm Poem: Jam Tree Gully, January 2018

The storm isn't here.
It isn't predicted. And yet
the barometer's
needle has cast its lot —

down past the leaf, even,
down to the floor —
all is stagnant, *no*, a tremble of door
& window, ants moving in —

I am withdrawn & extrovert,
making sure things are
secure. Nature is life, & a bout
of high wind and sparks stirs

us to friction — what can
be destroyed needs following
up with acts of conservation.
The storm is approaching —

no, it is always here,
building above & below us,
though skies remain clear.
No, the blue slightly feathers.

WE ASK MORE

Ask everything more of layout under pressure.
Ask for depths outside and maybe beyond sacred texts.

Reconfigure 'peace accords' in glyph-take from deficits
filling out coupons and decorations of hope — elope

in weather maps and tracking, diagrams and divinations.
Ask jam sessions to reconstitute your faith, to make

the dried stalks — wicks — of long dead orchids
to act as spectrometers in the shade of eucalyptus.

Ask more in circulars, gravity-fix of personality,
all those making monsters in snippets of bushland —

such machinery sits in sheds, comes out, deletes
a stretch of flooded gums, returns, settled down.

Ask further of here, ask to shed skin in quietude.
Think of how friendships can kindle in old gaols —

exhibits: chain & ball, inducing of claustrophobia
when that's a self-parody of the absurd: walls

already closed in, ticket of leave revoked in
striated light, and even back then gerygones,

pardelotes, prelates, roisterous mating song of rufous
whistler. Even then, as if, prayer for asking

to reset, play it differently, or *fait accompli*?
Never. Not in the hills of production, self-

sufficiency. Correlate a sea in the eye-drought!
What screech of epiphany dismissed for love?

We ask more under cloud where burn comes
fast and shockwave is no application — too

easy to see the disposition of incongruity
is setting up an image, phytochemical symbolism.

Why ask to ask more of core beliefs shed
when stress levels rise? To whom, and why?

Knowing more of *lore* than one should, it edges
under display, but can't be plumbed, scrutineers.

A leisure of worship, a relief of granite and clay,
of laterites fines to spread out as tracks to London

or Rome or even an *island* like Singapore. Television
reception is poor, and that's to be written as pyramid.

Here, further, out, nothing. Here asked of, a satellite
photographs as firebreaks glare, veins of geometry

leavened: heat signatures of *all life*, the beetle
we are surprised by (wherefore?), echidna gone

now from dead log ripped open, termite-less
city fallen out: after the event, the spiritual glossary?

Travel to define a feather's curve, its readiness
or unwillingness to wet or dry, precise place

of arising. Could be said simple as flight,
with interference from all directions. So,

allot this fragment to that erosion,
this *banging on about the same old thing*

to that poisoning. Some of it, honestly — epigene
you can't see grammatically, can't add to programme.

And a loop in a signature doesn't guarantee
cross reference, any more than echoing out

into marri flowerings makes ID — tinted snow
over hill bristles south of here, indeed *indeed!*, so

overwhelming that we'd believe the bunker-busting dozer
parked — snuggled — behind a few of them for over

a week now is *contrite*, pulling its head in,
lying low till (at least) the glorious palaver

of opening is over. Then *down down down*
into copyright and colonial overture of Underworld

idiom, a pew a cushion to kneel on, yank out weeds
in the old way (visions of ancient relatives?).

Ask more of a subject than an encyclopaedia
can offer you. Ask rubric and antiquity and transmutation,

ask gnosis and eitic/n-eitic/heitic/t-heitic & glory barbs
(a thumb is infecting from being scratched pulling caltrop).

Sore. Prayers lugged to carry you via — no way to obtain
lift when said and gone? Stirred in dust and residue

of manufacturing? Really, ask for more than shoot to kill
take aim at your denial of scorched earth? Your — *us* other:

'You gotta ask yourself, do you feel lucky, greenie punks?'
says the funny fairground fella, all pukka on Twitter.

We mean — commonplace, common prayer in league.
Such power quickfix laugh model stand-up massacre mirror.

It's all in the splurge, the burst of 'information'. Lamentations
are lamington drives to collate a backlash — the seedbank

(genetically modified) of moralising calls out moralists.
Pitchfork realism in tractor loveland, we bow down

and take our rolling back of vegetation on the chin-
wag. Wagtail does its watching, don't you worry. No fear!

Ask everything more of layout under pressure.
Ask more, ask more of jam sessions ask more

of nature descriptions ask more of annunciations
of erasure, ask more of art therapy and sacred texts.

AUTOBIOGRAPHY

'Come in, dead Emily.'
Judith Wright, 'Rosina Alcona to Julius Brenzaida'

All these lines we funnel, have need of.
The dead trouble us to live, and that can't
resolve into images that don't latch on
where ghosts wish for the tactile.
It's where I procured the word 'sullen',
and it inhabited or infected
or leavened my early poetry —
another (who?) victim of vocabulary, affect,
and compliance of syntax.
                 This open-sky
dungeon of colonial heritage — trapped
with the sea at your feet, even inland.
Such lovers as struggle in private games
only able to meet in lines stretched
out from natural materials, the machinery
of war and violence. It's all dispossession,
which makes the components no easier,
no more tolerable.
             Manufacturer's
default settings, our hands on the wheel,
these truck-heavy roads we risk our lives on,
adding to the complement of waste,
unravelling of flora and fauna.

Here, it's 'crimson fields'
and mock freedom.
                        The greatest song
ever written is June Carter Cash & Merle Kilgore's
'Ring of Fire' as sung by Johnny Cash — I knew
this at four, song recorded in my birth year,
and I listen to it now at Jam Tree Gully
fretting at world's end as the dry
invokes the burns with permits,
the fallout of dead rain,
knowing I have loved severely
and with ignition where fire must be suppressed
most of the year — where Tracy and I counter
our presence with prayers
neither of us tell each other.
                        What is this house
but a vast collection of books on a hillside —
a repository for the conversion of memories
into inanimate whispers we stir to life?
                        And
the fiery cunt of the world, the fury
of mating that made the spectra
and resisted the chains
that bankroll & ratify
the death cult of official
records.
            We don't really
need to know who Rosina Alcona
and Julius Brenzaida were, just stepping
out into an effusion of weebills & thornbills, ecstatic

with the possibility of rain four days from now,
measuring their lives in prospectus. We are fanatical
in ensuring no contamination from zone to zone —
so no Yorkshire moors soil is carried in on our shoes,
nor, really, in our heads, nor in the pages
of multiple editions of Emily's poems.
But Gondal resonates with sleep,
messing up the rigour.
     These poems
we made our way through,
whose lines remembered
come out at strange moments — moments
unaligned with what's *actually* going on,
rubbing up against ordinariness.
      We love
the complexity of magpie talk
       & interpretation
because interaction
     is so direct, intense —
the community
    redefining family for us, too: beaks
so perilous, they'd tear a 'demon's soul'
as much as the delicate songbird's
nestling.
   Early warning system —
to survive the threats we make
rhizomes in dirt & rock where moisture
is so deep bores are needed to bring it up:
but we leave it down there, surface
memories.

Each day eaten
by transport, by moving particles
across a spectrum of surge & exhaustion
& hope. Those trigger words
of critical faculties.
                    Emily,
obsession has nothing to do with themes
but everything to do with consistencies
only you and your collaborators
know. To break out
into the apostrophe, and refuse
medicaments.
                    Makes sense
to me as trees vanish across
the valley, excused by the contrivance
of calendars.
                    All of me, for what it's worth
outside the market economy, is in the shed
bark of the York gum — 'Yandee' if it's okay for me to say
(words can't be taken at a whim, but need to be earned
within the conceit I am working here — to be clear: the Noongar
peoples have the rights of their own language, and I'm
not infiltrating via the bullshit conventions
of making lines of verse) — and in the bronze
tending copper-green sheen beneath, the fresh treeskin
waiting for the next rough layer of growth,
                                    and those limitations
the English-language botanises. Emily, we're
stuck on the far sides
                    of the same synapses

in this. Me, anti-
royalist, lost in the miasma of empire: yours, sort of?
Its consequences?
                    No 'empty world'
to contain this pain, to fill with the effluvium
of being carried along by traffic, compelled
to move or perish.
                    Each day I study the wasps'
mud cells, made from dirt and fluid
though all our throats are dry.
Nothing marvellous in this — but
I have loved ones to tell, and that doesn't
obviate a spider's slow death
inside the darkness
where eggs hatch.
                    These stories
we tell to add up to a world
we might inhabit.
                    That's why:
thinking of the water tank
down to last rungs, and/or a small
repair job on a hole worn into the gravel
driveway — steep, narrated by ants.
That's why the call,
the reliance on where you've been
where you were. Are.

'THE MOON HAS SET'

via Emily Brontë

Such rights are set on texts
outside copyright, and that lake
is its own sphere of influence.
But we've had lakes in this house, too,
and your mother has each word
of the texts memorised, a glue
of psyche, a warm and comforting
water we swim through, out here, 'isolated'
though knowing there's so much more.
Venus shines close to the brink
of hills, the moon lifts nocturnal
animals, and the valley is a crater
lake filled with drought.
We never claim it as ours —
and there's no gentrification
of outlook. But we're here
till the building materials
let go, and its people
take it back. These lakes,
this dry, our imaginary
worlds with too little
or too much foothold.

RETRIEVAL

'Still as she looked the iron clouds
Would part and sunlight shone between
But drearily strange and pale and cold'
Emily Brontë

Even on a hot day it comes through cold.
Such reveries — processional caterpillars
retaining the line . . . the lead caterpillar
halts, they all halt. When from the night-
pile, the stacking up before dawn sets
them off, they head off in line a feeding
in takes place that no road network
could hope for. They share one signature
in the sand, slow-fast stable-unstable
emphatic, divisible and indivisible.
The pyrites coating the toe of the bank
still perplex and bother me, though I know
as much about their chemistry as you'd expect.
Fool's gold. A shimmering in full sun, but still
glittering on an overcast day. Always
the expectation of the sun busting
through. Iron is warfare. It is brass, too.
Maybe cannons captured at Waterloo
melted down and turned into bells.
The flow of triumphs. Trade winds.

And western quoll demand so much
territory to roam and hunt, maintaining
or counting on innumerable tree hollows
and burrows. Loners. And I reckon
one's got us in its range, and sunlight
broods oddly to underwrite or undercut
the point. These retrievals we can
so easily tire of — or reconfigure
the melancholy and confer
with what the sun has
to offer. Or collocates?

PSALM 139

Inside me you know.

You are present when I lie and when I rise; my thoughts are always
close to you.

You know my actions and my words; you know me inside out.

You know my speech entirely before it forms.

You surround me; you have touched me.

Such awareness is glorious and too glorious to reach.

Where can I look when you have seen all of me. Where can I hide?

If I enter heaven you will be waiting; if I sink to the lowest level
you will be there.

If I lift into the dawn, if I cross the vast sea,

you will accompany me, hold me tight with your right hand.

Should I call, 'I will be hidden in darkness and light will be a
cloak of night,'

darkness will be transparent, night will be as bright as day, for
darkness illuminates.

Who I am was made by you; you choreographed me inside my
mother's womb.

I am in awe because I live; because you have made me a miracle;
I know this.

You saw my shape form in the hidden world. When I was drawn in
the earth's depths,

you watched my shapelessness. All my days were preordained in
your book of life.

I hear your thoughts and cherish them. They are limitless!

They are more than the particles of existence. I wake to your
presence.

What am I to do with the wickedness? Away from me, you killers!
They exploit your name for violent ends; they profit from your
    glory.
Shouldn't I loathe those who mock all you stand for? Resist those
    who would damage?
I will not fall under their sway; I do not recognise their claims.
Examine my conscience, and know me; expose my deepest
    anxieties.
Extract my hypocrisies and guide me in eternal truth.

                                    a version by John Kinsella

The geographer Zenobius should have known better, Praxilla —
there is nothing 'feeble-minded' in equating the loss of crisp
    cucumbers,
pears and apples with the loss of the sun's beautiful light,
glimmer of the stars and glow of the moon's face.

The geographer Zenobius should have known better, Praxilla —
because Sicyon, your home city, was a bed of cucumbers,
and a vigorous celebrator of fruit trees and ripeness.
Cup in hand, looking out over the triangular plain, *you* knew love.

The geographer Zenobius should have known better, Praxilla —
knowing Adonis above and below ground, his skin venerating
his beauty, even in darkness, the memory of cucumbers
a guidebook to loss as even the best season will pass.

In the watery zone
the trees speak life-force

In the watery zone the trees speak life-force
against the loss, especially when the dry comes.
Fruits of marri trees stock the skies, but the red
and orange tail-flashes of cockatoos coming in to roost
are short-circuited by the sudden, brutal absence.

And so many years ago stands of rivergums were planted,
having grown and added to the slimmed-pickings, to add body
to spaces hacked up, providing refuge for these long-lived birds.
Now to be felled and fibred — a mockery. Trees that take the
     watery force
into birdsleep between sky and earth, raucous and vibrant.

'Reshaped', it won't grow fast enough as the canopy-world
is deleted across the coastal plain. And developers don't *get*
the interlinked destinies of wet ground and vegetation, of Yule
and Crystal Brooks and precinct and vicinity — nor consequence.
The edge of the wetlands is still the wetlands and the buffer

is each step you take over what was, because it still *is*, and connects.
Today, walking the edges of the Brixton Street Nature Reserve, not
     wanting
to go too deep in because quenda and bobtails, native bees and
     butcher birds,
need places beyond our steps given what's left, we knew the silent
     drinking
of the redbreast bush, and the wodjalok sliding from marri branch
     down fast

to yellow wattle bloom, while the passed-cold-wet-months of
    sign-bearing froglets'
prime time, and yellow buttercups tracking the light for
    suggestions
of flower-loving insects, were cross-talked by dragonfly angles,
    abrupt
over the buff waters of pools tuned by melaleucas, nymphs of
    other cycles
close to the surface which something sprints across into shadow,

a native grass tree offering fresh flower spikes — the kind of
    sustainable
development the wetlands know about. Bobtail eating flowers
    to glow
from the inside out is a joy no heavy earth-moving equipment
    can recognise,
nor the drawers of precinct maps — not really. We can live within
    this moment
remaining from before the exploitation — we can cross, too, if
    we're careful.

We all need somewhere to land, to eat, to deliberate and envision
    lives,
but not where the cockatoos eat and sleep, not where carnivorous
    plants thrive.

ACKNOWLEDGEMENTS

'The Bulldozer Poem' has appeared in various capacities, including in the book *On the Outskirts* (University of Queensland Press, 2017) and can be seen being read here: https://www.youtube.com/watch?v=Xhf 2dRlUbVU. This poem can be used freely for pro-environmental purposes. 'Milking the Tiger Snake' and 'Hiss' were originally published in the *New Yorker*. 'Sea Lion', 'Resurrection of the Kerry Bog Ponies', 'Bat! in Tübingen, Late Winter', and 'Graphology Mutation 25: the authenticity of ploughing' originally appeared in the *Times Literary Supplement*. 'Shark Tale Paradox' appeared in the *West Australian Newspaper*. 'Hymn for Giant Creeper Snails and their Shells', 'Swan Chevrons', and 'Graphology Soulaplexus 25: hover fly' originally appeared in *Artful Dodge*. 'Wagenburg' and 'Searching for the Tübingen Friedenseiche (Peace Oak)' originally appeared in the *Boston Review of Books*. [Regarding quote used in this poem, see: http:// http://www.waymarking.com/waymarks/ WMGK0J_Friedenseiche_Peace_Oak_Tbingen_Germany_BW.] 'Mute Swans Over Carraiglea' was published in the book *Marine* (with Alan Jenkins; Enitharmon Press, 2015). 'Post-Traumatic' and 'Grey Heron is Not a Hood Ornament' appeared in *Cyphers*. 'Fingerprints Lacking in Bantry' appeared in *New Humanist*. 'Sizing Up Cape Clear Island with a Trigger Thumb' originally appeared in the *Colorado Review*. 'Charolais' was published in *Five Points*. 'Wren's Electric Field Strength' and 'Zoo' were published in *Australian Poetry Journal*. 'Hay-Baling Realisation of Space Over Place' and '"Buzz Pollination"' were published in *Meanjin*. 'Emily Brontë Storm Poem' was published in the *Australian*. My Emily poems are collectively dedicated to Tim Dolin. 'Graphology Endgame

100: I am a dickhead' was published in the *Australian Book Review*'s 'States of Poetry'. 'Graphology Symptomatic 4: Floribunda' is from the book *Graphology Poems 1995–2015* (volume III; Five Islands Press, 2016). 'Borromini's Perspective and the Galleria Spada's Resident Cat' appeared in *Spiralling* (Newton Institute of Mathematics, Cambridge, 2017). 'Orange 1962 Massey Ferguson Tractor' and 'Red' first appeared in the *Kenyon Review* and 'The Bonfire of Vanities' in *Southern Review*. 'In the water zone trees speak life-force' can be used as a pro-environmental support poem without permission — it was originally written in support of the 'Save Brixton Street Wetland and the Kenwick roost' (ongoing) campaign, and published in *WA Today*, the *Sydney Morning Herald* and the *Canberra Times*. Other poems appeared in *Agni*, the *Denver Quarterly*, the *Griffith Review*, and *Literary Imagination*. Special thanks to Tracy Ryan, my partner, our son Tim, and the rest of my family. Also to Don, Kish, and the editors of publications listed above. Thanks also to Curtin University where I am Professor of Literature and Environment, and a Curtin Fellow, as well as to Churchill College, Cambridge University, which has long been a special zone for me. I also acknowledge the Ballardong Noongar people whose land I often write, and most often live on.